The Light Box places the personal alongside classic myths, the imagined lives, and afterlives, of ordinary people, cultural icons, and those depicted in their art. Stanley Spencer, Margaret Thatcher, two men kissing in an airport arrivals hall; in Rosie Jackson's hands, 'the ordinary becomes unfamiliar and scarred with legend'.

Rosie Jackson works with creative writing and the arts in community and health settings. She has degrees from Warwick and York, has taught at the University of East Anglia, and is widely published. She lives near Frome in Somerset.

www.rosiejackson.org.uk

It's a long time since I was so enchanted with a body of poems; these haunt my imagination with their deft sleights-of-hand, shifting personae, lightly-handled depths of wit, heart-intelligence, compassion, perceptiveness. They intrigue, seduce, move, invite question. What gives Jackson's work its strength and rarity is her merging of the numinous with the power of the sensory world.

Roselle Angwin, author of
All The Missing Names Of Love

Stonking good poems.

Jo Bell, author of *Kith*

The Light Box expertly explores the territory of both heart and spirit. Confidently crafted poems, by turns intimate and expansive, bring together emotional authenticity and sparkling imagination. A richly rewarding collection.

Stephen Boyce, author of *The Sisyphus Dog*

Detail after stunning detail exposes rapture, fear, longing. These poems will make your battered heart beat fast again.

Claire Crowther, author of *Silents*

THE LIGHT BOX

Other books by the author

What the Ground Holds (Poetry Salzburg, 2014)

Frieda Lawrence: Including "Not I, But the Wind"
(Harper Collins/Pandora List, 1994)

*Mothers Who Leave: Behind the Myth of Women without Their
Children* (Harper Collins/Pandora List, 1994)

The Eye of the Buddha and Other Therapeutic Tales
(Women's Press, 1991)

Fantasy: The Literature of Subversion
(Routledge, 1981)

THE LIGHT BOX

ROSIE JACKSON

Cultured Llama Publishing

First published in 2016 by
Cultured Llama Publishing
11 London Road
Teynham, Sittingbourne
ME9 9QW
www.culturedllama.co.uk

Copyright © 2016 Rosie Jackson

ISBN 978-0-9932119-7-3

Printed in Great Britain by Lightning Source UK Ltd

Cover design by Lyn Davies Design

Front cover painting by Stanley Spencer (1891–1959): 'The
Resurrection: Reunion', 1945, reproduced by kind permission
of Aberdeen Art Gallery and Museums, and the Spencer estate
© The Estate of Stanley Spencer/Bridgeman Images.

Author photograph by Gordon McKerrow

Contents

Author's Note

In 2011, I had a short residency at Cheltenham Art Gallery and Museum (now The Wilson), which focused on painting by the visionary English artist Stanley Spencer (1891–1959).

My fascination with Spencer's art and life led to several poems about Spencer and his complicated relationship with first wife, artist Hilda Carline; these poems preface each of the six sections of *The Light Box*.

The front cover shows the right panel of Stanley Spencer's triptych 'The Resurrection: Reunion', 1945, the painting that inspired 'Resurrection', the final poem in *The Light Box*. All the other Spencer paintings mentioned, as well as art and artists referred to in other poems, can be found online.

I didn't trust it for a moment,
but I drank it anyway,
the wine of my own poetry.

It gave me the daring to take hold
of the darkness and tear it down
and cut it into little pieces.

Lalla (1320–1392), *Naked Song*,
translated by Coleman Barks

1. Love's Exuberance

Touch Paper
after Stanley Spencer's 'Love Letters', 1950

Your words pressed tight
against my chest
till my skin burns
as if this paper
that has touched your body
been breathed on
by your breath
held close against your heart
beneath your flowered dress
carries the fire of the sun
in its great script
of longing
of excess
of perfect love
brought down to earth
made flesh
made womanly
made you.

Oh love letters
sweet heart letters
how short-sighted I've become
in my love of you
reading the lines so closely
heat rising on pages
milled from beech and pine
and river that you
slipping the next envelope
into my jacket pocket
are nothing but a blur
a muse without whose
words I cannot live

cannot breathe unless
you write me again
promise me
there is no future
without this writing in it.

What Their Books Yield

The carnation: a wedding buttonhole
pressed into sepia, wafer-thin,
between the pages of Gibbon's *Decline and Fall*.

Frayed edges of birthday cards, bus tickets,
black and white photos, torn Rizla, notes,
quotes copied out in his copperplate script.

A ribbon marking her favourite sonnet,
an oil stain where, impatient to know who did it,
he forgot to wash the grease from his hands.

This folded-over corner because here it was
her soul first quickened to poetry,
the hurried turning her hunger for the light.

That squiggle in the margin in *The End of the Affair*,
the asterisk, the tide mark where they walked on water,
the fervent pencilled full capitals *YES!*

So many pages opening like French windows
onto unexpected afternoons:
he reading out loud to himself,

she to the stranger just out of sight.
Their love of words, their cherished lines,
the imprint of their touch, their sleepless nights.

First Breakfast

And I want to push aside the chairs,
the plates, the daffodils,
to hold his face in my hands,
bite his lip, pour into his mouth
my secret joy, my jug of prayer,
my wild gestures, the jars of love
I've been saving for years. Then words,
milked for their yellow shining,
and silence, the music in me that can't be heard,
I want to pour that too, the liquid gold,
the steadfast amber there are no thoughts for.

Whatever I have of light
goes into him; whatever I knew of dark
shrugged away. Everything changed
in this epiphany as we face each other,
life against life, heart against heart,
in this moment of yes –
joy, rain, skin, kisses.
And outside, in the cold salt world,
old maps in turmoil, lustrous new rivers.

Airport Kiss

These are mouths that have been waiting
for months to meet on the same continent,
and they kiss without shame,
drawing us all in as we watch
over our stale Starbucks,
sharing that taste of coffee
tart and bitter on the lover's tongue
and smelling minty toothpaste
from that hurried cleaning
3,000 feet above, that in-flight
dab of aftershave,
wondering how long it can last
this one-breath kiss
between two men,
one slender, suited, black, neatly professional,
the other with bare arms toned to stone
and buttocks tight in frayed denims,
while the rest of us shuffle
to greet our own tame passengers,
British enough to know
how to pretend to look away,
while keeping one envious eye
fixed on love's exuberance.

The Lovers' Exchange

He traces the scar on her knee, indigo still
from the playground's coal dust and gravel.
She wonders at the small V over his heart:
a girlfriend's angry scissors.
The marks on her wrist he passes over silently,
touches the hollow of a lost child.
Lets her caress the scorch on the back of his hand
from when he was eight, an English boy living
in Germany, and the man in the barber's shop
stubbed his cigarette in the young white flesh,
said: *That's for Dresden.*
She puts her lips to that place
where the fires burn all these years on,
as if her mouth, her one breath,
were enough to blow out the candles of war,
return to their bodies newborn skin
on which nothing is written.

That Night of Her Honeymoon

she remembers what Freud said about sex:
how it's not two people in bed, but six –

the couple themselves, his parents, then hers;
and, no doubt, a whole mob of ancestors

pouring in like ghosts through the hotel walls,
wanting to taste again the rituals

of which they were particularly fond.
This unfamiliar way her husband

pulls her hair – not violent, but sharper –
is probably the way his grandfather

claimed his fiancée after his long years
of waiting. And her own hunger for this

man beside her, the new way she's taking
him, as if they were once field-hands coupling

as her parents did under a harvest
moon. Here are women with her blood who lost

babies, who want to see her own take root,
to watch over its entry, play some part

in this greatest pleasure they know, calling
a soul to earth – and here's her son falling

now at the speed of light into her womb,
one of the rare ones – sure of love, welcome.

Not Minding What Happens

If you could unhitch yourself from your DNA,
like a train leaving behind wrong carriages;

if you could be as open as a doorway unafraid
of thieves, not needing to see the invisible colour

to know there is a miracle; if you could unhook
from knowing better than life – or death – what's good

for you and your close ones; then sometimes,
in the middle of the afternoon, when you're walking

through a wet field, the wall might fall from the side
of the world, and a golden light hit you like a sudden field

of rape. Then words of complaint, prayer, beseeching,
will dive into the grass and rise again as larks singing,

the light being so bright, so all you didn't know you
   craved,
so making up for every loss, unsayable.

Darkness With Excess of Light

Love papers the world with roses, leaves,
thorns we can see through.
We slip our bodies' thick black lines.
Colours trespass on the grass.

No tentative sketches now,
only this defiance:
hearing the waves cry, tidemarks
laying new shores at our feet.

Leaving each other in the morning
poised for difference,
the day a box that never closes,
paradise pressing against our backs.

And when darkness returns, it is nothing
but a blanket tossed half-heartedly
towards our radiance,
helpless to eclipse this clear white ground.

Sketchbook

The earth in pencil, improvised, one tree
after another drawn from the blank page.
A whole thicket emerging out of doubt.

One line carves out a branch, a bole, a copse,
then turns to summon stump and Domesday Oak.
A spike of hawthorn, loop of mistletoe.

Here's snow where shadows lift back into light.
A smudge of crows. A surge of dashes
sudden rain lashing the morning sideways.

He's not drawing the one tree or the bird
but the slow fugue between them and the wind –
wood and wing registering the difference

between bark and feather. Time's on this bench
watching for flights of goldfinch, tit, fieldfare.
These small black marks equal green woodpeckers.

Here's conifers I walked by yesterday,
these hasty scrawls my boots and anorak,
my feet in mud, a smell of pine needles.

And where the graphite's gently rubbed away
until the paper's almost white again
that moment when the winter sun broke through.

Barbara Hepworth Considers the Visitors at Trewyn

They love to ask about the fire:
those scorch marks on my living room floor.

Or they sit in the garden hoping
an angel might appear

looking like me – red gingham scarf,
a chisel behind each ear.

The holes are where we meet –
for them, a weightless place of possibilities,

for me, the hollow of what's missed –
the inside edge of stone, unpolished bronze,

sounds like the mirage of sea inside
a shell – an ocean of far-off moments.

And I want to tell them it's as true now:
there is no fixed point

of light – everything still asks
to be touched, walked through.

The Light Box

Moths, of course, don't make the news.
Not unless you follow Chuck on Twitter:
fine in the fire and feeds on friction,
who wants to know, *why there are so many*
fucking moths in Afghanistan?
Or Google the latest research on turning
Tobacco Hawks into cyborg spies,
implanting larvae with microchips
so their soft little bodies will harden into drones,
enter enemy camps as light-winged innocence.

But there are men near Kandahar
who hand their children magnifying glasses
to marvel at exotic marks on Sphingid moths;
men whose heads touch the earth
five times each day in gratitude, awe, humility:
Bismillah ir-Rahman ir-Rahim.

Men like my neighbour, who shows me
his old-fashioned biscuit tin
transformed into a light box,
where moths squat like refugees
on egg boxes.

Men who catalogue species
so they won't die out unheeded,
then release them at dawn:
Mother of Pearl, Cinnabar,
Scalloped Oak, Six-Spot Burnet,
Peppered Geometer.

Men we never hear of,
who keep alive
the light box in their hearts.
Attract nightly visitations.

2. So Many Spoons

Hilda Carline Spencer

after Stanley Spencer's 'Village Life', 1940

You can't see my face properly.
I'm like that tree by the far fence,
falling out of the frame.
He's looking down too,
abashed, perhaps, at how he treated me.
Linked by our sorrow,
both of us miss what's happening in the sky,
barely listening to the child
who can see what we can't –
her signpost finger pointing
to the skies' opening,
the radiance coming through,
even the washed shirts rising
like the undergarments of angels.

Advice from Georges de la Tour

Always pay attention
to the source of light:
candle, taper, sun, window.

Include the beating heart,
the woman whose back aches as I paint her,
who dreams of fish and loaves for supper.

Capture red, ochre, sandstone,
the scarlet of ripe haws,
the knowing lips of the Magdalene.

But make all this convey that other light,
the one behind all others,
the only reason to pick up a brush,

catch a smile, preserve moments
of love, of loss, epiphany – the quiet
presence of unacknowledged fire.

Spoons

after a display of 17th-century silver spoons, Holburne Museum, Bath

So many spoons hanging in the glass case
So many tongues licking the tarnished spoons
So many meats enticing the forked tongues
So many cooks roasting the bloody meats
So many dawns startling the roosting cooks
So many nights dying to sleepless dawns
So many footfalls treading through raw nights
So many ears hearing secret footfalls
So many words worming through artless ears
So many kisses peddling for sweet words
So many hearts swinging on thin kisses
So many glasses drinking broken hearts
So many spoons stirring the cut glasses
So many mouths mooning for silver spoons

Could You Make My Mouth Smile More?

Sitting to have my portrait drawn,
everything goes back to that night when I was four:
sneaking downstairs through the dark, meeting a stranger
in the lamplight, where I'd expected to find my mother.
Lying in this young woman's lap, drawings of bodies:
baby, gorgeous from all angles,
hands, arms, legs, a nude – my first.
And what a wondrous likeness of me: my tousled curls,
my sleeping child's mouth half open, hungry for the world.
This was the woman I wanted to be: unafraid of nakedness.
How did I get to be a magician who conjured up a person
out of nothing? Who made this child? What was this secret
of lines and shapes, this mystery of creating life?
If I could do what she had done, lost in a trance
of deft flesh on white space, I would no longer be alone,
never again without this company –
shoulders, eyebrows, ankles, knees, kisses –
a mother joined to her baby in one line.
That night I fell in love, vowed I would be her,
able to magic away absence. Remembering,
I ask the artist to make my mouth smile a little more –
sitting for my new portrait,
legs crossed, shoulders slightly hunched,
a perfect rose on my jacket.

A perfect rose on my jacket,
legs crossed, shoulders slightly hunched,
sitting now for my new portrait,
I ask the artist to make my mouth smile a little more,
able to magic away absence. Remembering
that night I fell in love, vowed I would be her:
a mother joined to her baby in one line –

shoulders, eyebrows, ankles, knees, kisses –
never again without this company
of deft flesh on white space. I would no longer be alone,
if I could do what she had done, lost in a trance
of lines and shapes, this mystery of creating life
out of nothing. Who made this child? What was this secret?
How did I get to be a magician who conjured up a person?
This was the woman I wanted to be, unafraid of nakedness,
my sleeping child's mouth half open, hungry for the world.
And what a wondrous likeness of me: my tousled curls,
hands, arms, legs, a nude – my first
baby gorgeous from all angles,
lying in this young woman's lap. Drawings of bodies
in the lamplight, where I'd expected to find my mother
sneaking downstairs through the dark, meeting a stranger.
Everything goes back to that night when I was four,
sitting to have my portrait drawn.

Wanting to Write About Happiness Is to

stand in a beehive up to your neck in pollen
watch the afternoon unpack its yellowness
layer upon layer

brush fig leaves from your breasts
twist towards a sky no longer stained with smoke
lean into a wind as solid as birdsong

rise like Venus as ready for the past
as for the future
undo the pewter rings of certainty

feel the world under your fingertips
like Braille waiting to be deciphered
into the language of joy

make words part of the silence
this book of solid yellow on yellow
this earth drenched in honeycomb

The Desire to Be Porcelain
after the Witcombe Cabinet, 1697, Holburne Museum, Bath

This is wood trying to better itself,
to skim over its knotted English grain
a lacquered vision of Japan:
bees with no stings, skies without shadow,
a geisha's world of flower and willow.

My mother would have loved it here,
the roped-off beauty.
Museums were her church –
hushed air, sweet smell of floor polish.
This yellowing would be her window
to a sunlit Gloucestershire estate,
where she too wakes in velvet, walks
through pear trees, feathers in her hair,
works tapestries with tulips, *fleurs-de-lis*.

But I ask questions of locked drawers –
imagine dropped gloves, blooded keys,
an *Old Moore's Almanac*;
mistrust an art that turns trees into porcelain,
spurns the heartwood they once were,
disguises one thing as another.

The First Men of Light

I've seized the light! I've arrested its flight!
Daguerre in Paris, 1839 –
his *Boulevard du Temple*, its tall white
houses rising like spectres, soft skyline
of a ghostly city. The exposure
of his photo so long, it can define
only motionless things on the silver-
plated copper. Traffic, horses and crowd
that afternoon fled into the ether.
But two small figures persist: one a proud
Parisian, standing as the other
kneels in front of him – a bootblack, head bowed,
the first ghost to be caught on camera,
condemned to be in service forever.

Picasso at the Café de Flore

He is a master contortionist:
knows how to slide eyes
halfway down a cheek,
split faces in two. But still
it startles him when the reflection
in the café window –

his own, the short but robust male
women fall for – hesitates,
then remains standing when he
sits down, watching him
like a stubborn lover
who refuses to be dismissed.

He turns his back, soaks up sunlight
from the Boulevard Saint-Germain,
tries not to glance round
and see the self in the glass
hanging there
like a detached retina.

Even when he saunters away
he remains confused,
drunk beyond anything
he's consumed, confounded
which of them is real
and which the absence.

And for a while that day,
he too – the great master
of division – is caught
in the same space his models
occupy, somewhere
between canvas and sky.

My Uncle Visits Mt Vesuvius, 1944

He doesn't see it as sublime, this mountain
of lava, magma. Doesn't read the clouds
as shadowed angels holding up the light.

He hasn't come to paint. Has no retinue
of easel carriers, no evening wine above the Bay
of Naples. Only the war has brought him here.

I think of him, in front of Joseph Wright's
Eruption of Vesuvius, the rivers of red fire
halted by a placid pewter tide.

What the canvas can't capture is the smell
of sulphur, saltpetre, the sticky tar
that coats men's lungs like coal dust back home.

I don't know who carried his body –
there were no fathers or brothers left.
Only my mother and hers to stand

like these grieving Marys shrouded
in Wright's dim foreground. Nearby, two men bear
a barefoot third upon their shoulders, stoop

as if death has made his youth as heavy
as a cross. Mum stayed puzzled by the loss.
She kept his spectacles on the sideboard for years.

The Letter Cutter
for Andrew Whittle

You have carved them so many times,
these dates that sit before and after.

You know the best texts, the forms,
the letters *sans serif*, unyielding capitals.

You have stood so often on this threshold
of the other world like an Egyptian bird,

broad-shouldered, dark, you must know
something of the mystery –

something of what remains of a man
beyond these ceremonial bookends.

Day after day you hammer home the stone
to just the right depth in just the right spot

for these characters of love
to catch the light.

Undoing

And what if, each morning, after another sleepless night,
Penelope takes herself down to the edge of the sea,
to the place where she was last happy,
that moment before Odysseus stepped
into the treacherous surf, too eager to unstick
from land, from her.

And what if she knows he won't come back,
the man she knew, that the absence round which
she has stitched and unstitched so repeatedly
will be impossible to fill, and even after his return
will live on as a ghost inside
her husband's weather-beaten skin.

And what if, these twenty years grounded
on Ithaca, she has been haunted
by invisible landscapes quite as compelling
as the one that plunged Odysseus
into the undertow, perfection
that does not translate easily into form.

And what if her addiction to undoing is more,
far more, than a wife's extravagant patience,
this nightly unpicking of the day's yes
an artist's fidelity to what eludes,
the dark hours a ritual admission of failure;
these once golden now frayed and grubby silks

her sign of hunger for what can be known
only by its absence, a something – like love,
she tends to think now, like perfect love –
which lets itself come close only when she unravels
what falls short, lets itself be known
as desire, exile, longing.

Recovery Stroke

after Grainger McKoy's sculpture 'Recovery Wing', 2010

How heavy it seems, this duck in flight,
wing down and flattened, not knowing

if it will have the strength to pull up again,
waiting for the next push forwards,

a divine acrobat – comical at times –
stuck on the wall in threes

as if there is something quite absurd,
ridiculous, about a duck in flight –

but look at its beauty:
every feather and tendon

used to the maximum in its rotation
of back and forth, up and down,

knowing without being told
that moving forward

requires a moving back,
that no stroke is wasted –

that the greatest beauty sometimes
happens at the weakest point.

3. The Difference Between Them

The Apple Gatherer

after Stanley Spencer divorced Hilda to marry Patricia Preece – a marriage that was never consummated – he persuaded Hilda to be his lover

I was the first wife,
the one who flew to earth
with strong wrists that could paint for hours,
nurse a child, turn a mangle.
I gathered seeds in my artist's smock,
the best windfalls.

But she had scissors in her pocket,
clipped my babies' wings,
taught us all to drink vinegar.
And when she became the second wife,
I, wishing my hips to be brash like hers,
agreed to be the mistress.

He said he was married to us both,
bugger the law, love was bigger.
Now I don't know which ring belongs where,
whether to be jealous of myself or her,
who's the mother of these step-children,
whose heart is barren.

I lie down in Cookham's orchards,
look up at apple trees he painted
when we lived in heaven.
Try to remember where I came from,
swallow my own forked tongue,
watch cyanide turn slowly into blossom.

What A Wife Is For

I want to see her as she was
when she was still his newness,
this woman
with green eyes,
her cropped copper hair
the gleam of a freshly minted coin.

I want to wipe the tears before she cries them,
to not let her face, elfin even now,
darken as she walks into a forest
with nothing but dead needles on the floor,
a stillness in the air saying all she cares for
has been eaten by wolves.

I want to say to her husband,
her husband who is about to leave her,
don't do it, remember the being-in-love you felt with her too,
your three babies she visited death to retrieve,
the heft it took to lift them from her body,
the twenty-year patience with which she's cherished them.

I want to tell him he is killing the world,
that because of him hummingbirds will die,
the earth will fall into cracks,
morning glory lose its blue,
angels will raise their swords against him,
his children's rage will harden into stones.

I want him to get it. But the smell
of a younger woman's on his skin,
his hunger a lurcher straining on its leash.
What is the prospect of his wife's forever grief

compared to some fresh girl who *understands*,
who makes him feel his life can *start anew?*

I don't pull away the linen cloth,
don't tell what they don't know yet,
these twelve guests around the table, waiting to be fed;
want her to have one last perfect evening,
pass the plates, unfold my napkin,
watch her fingers breaking bread.

In Which I Liken Our Ending to Masaccio's 'Expulsion'

Her hand grieving for the space between her legs.
His sex naked, unabashed even in its fall.
Her breasts tender, knowing
they will never be touched that way again.
His pain gone into his head, behind his eyes,
trying to work his way through something
as incalculable as loss.
Her mouth open in a cry that lasts for centuries.
How will they live in the sand
without fountains, branches, birdsong?
Unable to lift their heads towards the hem
of the red angel who has raised his sword.
Unable to bear the memory of the bliss
they have squandered.
He wanting to blame her for being forward,
hungry, climbing trees.
She lamenting with her body what is gone.
They do not touch. They do not speak.
The first woman, the first man.
Already the difference between them.

On Not Being Able to Remember My Wedding Dress

My middle marriage, I mean –
not the first, in a maroon crepe dress
with patent leather shoes; nor the third,
in a raw silk suit of nacreous pink,
new high heels to match –
but the piggy-in-the-middle one
that urban rainy day in spring.
I can recall details of delivery vans –
the urgent sound they made reversing –
our feet stepping round petrol puddles, witnesses
from the street, his over-theatrical promises.
And the two golden bands I'd bought
then pocketed again six months later,
when I filed for divorce. But what I wore
remains a mystery – a little black number
perhaps? Leather skirt? Pearls? Taffeta?
Velvet? Denim? Suede? Something on loan
from folly, anyway, size zero –
with nothing underneath but lace, suspenders,
stockings from a little French place.

From Your Uncoy Mistress
after Andrew Marvell and T.S. Eliot

We're heading for landfill, darling,
from the moment we're born – falling –
and you don't know how quick that fall
can be – a sudden curtain call
that arrives unexpectedly
while we're writing our poetry,
counting lives in spoon and metre.
Come to me, there's nothing better
than being in each other's skin.
Think only of rising, rising –
we'll go without sleep, you and I,
while dawn spreads out against the sky.
As for my not being so young,
ignore gossip's evergreen tongue –
why shouldn't an older woman
make wild love with a younger man?
And he with me? Such convention
about age needs to be undone.
        I'm sure of one thing: patriarchs
know nothing of the kind of sex
we can enjoy – love that strikes sparks
to light up the enduring dark.
So come to me now, now, before
the body rolls up its trousers,
loses sight, loses mind. Come, trust
this passion, this love, this great lust
for life. We must make memories
for that lonely night when we cross
bitter sands where our souls will drift
without touch or kiss. Come, be swift,
the future's snapping at our feet.

And if death reaches for my coat,
throw back at him our nakedness,
our kisses, our eternal YES.
Say: life's overwhelming answer
is love over death, forever
love – this is all we can retrieve
from time, this is all we can leave.
Come to me, let me take your youth
in my arms, kiss your lovely mouth
this white-haired morning. Come, be quick,
brand me with love so when flames lick
round my body, I'll remember
nothing but this you-and-I fire,
this untethered pleasure, this rough
sweetness worth being human for.

As Your Wife

The day they put your father in a box,
everything went horizontal –
words scored through
with a thick black line.
You even became sentimental
behind the hearse,
gripping my arm tighter
than you'd held it before,
as if being your wife gave me
some charm that kept at bay
the curse of all you feared.
More tender than I'd ever heard,
you whispered, *Someday one of us
will have to do this for the other.*
But now your ashes are thrown
into the wind on Dartmoor
by a woman I've never met.
And I'm remembering your mother's grief
that night of your father's death:
how my guilt grew extravagant
at our togetherness –
as if our love too had found a tunnel
we could not live and enter.

Getting to Unknow You

When you come to me in my dreams you're doing
things we did together – hauling stones, building walls –
or bent over the land as though unearthing
what led to your error. Will I ever unlearn the intimacy of you?
Lift my head from your chest, unhear your heart beating
its metronome of tenderness into my ear? Your presence
is so strong that when I wake I find your hair
on my pillow, as if you were trying to comfort, remind me
that our marriage was the backbone of our lives,
gave us strength to walk through it all, even all the loss of it.
You appear night after night, wanting to undo the mesh
of retrospective pain in which our years together are now
    caught –
the way your faithlessness sours all that went before, throws
bitterness over those early kisses, summer picnics,
stepping-stone love. Perhaps we all wander out
under cover of sleep into the vast underworld of dreams,
visit hearts we've damaged in our turn, say
things we should have said, make love in ways
we always longed for. Perhaps it is I who summon you
in these corridors of unknowing, needing to forget,
yet secretly appeased to brush against you in the crowd
    of souls,
trying their hardest to undo, unpick, unhurt.

The Girl Who Had No Life Insurance

was stopped by police
for walking
on the hard shoulder

drank instant coffee
with three heaped teaspoons
of questions

planted a yellow rose
in a bucket
of water

told them the story
of a woman
with no tongue

After the Separation

Hard to get used to no upstairs; his two girls
in the bedroom next door squashed together
like dormice. Half the time his lungs breathe air:

he helps with homework, cooks, buys bargain orchids
for the lounge. The other half, when the girls
are with their mother in the house he bought –

its spaciousness, a bed imprinted
with her lover's limbs –
he's at the bottom of the sea, stuck

in a watery strangeness. Urchins and sand dollars
shift inside his skin. Anger would help,
but grief keeps the touch paper wet.

Wakes not knowing where he is, pulse too fast;
wanting to push out the walls. A thin-lipped
dawn sidles over the bungalow lawn;

prayer flags of laundry pegged to the line.
Needing to believe, for his girls' sake, love will win.
Needing to remain a man worth living in.

Blood Moon

We were balanced on the head of a pin,
the light behind closed doors strong enough
to open everything, lay bare our skin,
throw radiance to the back of the house

like those silver trays held by servants
at mouths of caves in India, bouncing
the sun so deep into the dark, cutters
could carve the most perfect *Bodhisattva*.

Then came the eclipse: that red moon rolling
fire over the ocean, and here you are,
earth's shadow, walking to me from your car
on autumn leaves, your face implacable,

nothing but friends, as you shake love away,
hand back my key, take down our bright sky.

Had We Known

when you climbed into bed with wet hair
that night, we would have memorised
the poems we read, looked at each other
longer, burned the retina.

But we never know it is the last time
before it happens, walking out and out
next morning on flat grey sands,
the tide already fled.

And now, unwittingly, thousands upon
thousands are doing these same things –
kissing mouths they will not meet again,
drinking from cups they will no longer share,

the exodus sudden –
marriages squashed into rucksacks,
babies into pockets,
thoughts of prey as absolute as death

hanging over them
like those dark birds Nostradamus prophesied
arriving from the east,
the shadow of their forked wings

spreading into Europe –
leaving beds empty, temples without gods,
unlove spilling its cargo
along motorways and fields.

None of us could see this coming:
crowds on the move, bodies in the jungle,
heads needing pillows,
our unready laps.

4. I Too Saw The Skies Open

Seated Nude
after Stanley Spencer's 'Portrait of Hilda', 1942

It's an awkward study,
the light playing over me
as if I were sitting under a trellis –
beautiful but sad –
my flesh serene in its mortality.

Nipples erect, but only with the cold.
There is no lust,
none of the meaty pleasure
that reddens his portraits of Patricia.
My hips discreet,
my body haunted by promises
given then kissed away.

I allowed it all to happen
because I too saw the skies open,
the graves spilling their dead,
the veil of the temple rent.
Few painters can capture that, but he did.

Not me. I had babies instead – his –
and now my body is an empty vessel.
Please cover it.
Place a blanket over me.

He writes to me now, says he wants me back,
but the separation has settled around me
like silence I've grown used to.
My anger squashed like pressed flowers.
The flesh around my waist puckered.

Mary Shelley, Hyde Park, 1850

She tries to avoid the Serpentine, but today
it's on her before she's aware: a mouth that doesn't close,
green water pulling her.

Not that she cares for reflections any more,
her hair grown thin, the skin on her face slack,
as if carelessly stitched.

Always fighting to keep the membrane intact,
to stop the dead pushing through,
not see her baby in these carriages in the park,

not remember the feel of her husband's collarbone
inside his open-necked shirt,
the drum of his heart under naked ribs.

But now her hand has reached into the lake,
found Harriet as she lies there,
drifting under the surface like pondweed.

And when Harriet's fingers stick to hers,
she doesn't prise them away, but nods: *Yes,*
I was the one who stole your young husband,

I was the one who stole lightning from the gods
and made a man. And they took away my marriage,
its angels of rain and light, and child after child in return.

The trees are white, everything in London white.
The pavement, turned to ice, cracks underfoot
and bodies lie in the ocean beneath her; ropes; oars; tiny
    bones.

She pulls up her collar. *How tame I have become,*
shrinking from the west wind. Is this what grief has done?
Left me on the side of shadows? And when she sits to write,

the words are snow and cannot warm her,
even her quiet moments too full of apocalypse.
This is how it is when the world has no mother.

I'll Never Live in a Lighthouse

though I often
dream of standing
where the earth is
pulled away from
under my feet and
I'm reprieved
from landlock,
wanting to believe
the promise of the
sea to dissolve the
horizon. I too
hurry towards it
year after year
with windbreaks,
surfboards, bare
legs, losses,
wanting to
recapture what
I'm made of,
swim seal deep,
backstroke my life
into the first
surrender, that
blue swell where
turquoise tips to
pewter then to
water that is no
colour at all.

Night Sky

We never thought to learn the names of stars.
They were just places light once found a home.

But now you're gone, I need to know
which one you've become. Are you

hidden in Lupus, Orion, Cassiopeia?
Perched like an egret on the back of Pegasus?

Flying to Pyxis, Equuleus? Kissing the Seven Sisters?
Is it their love you're coaxing into being now?

Tell me, so I can aim my telescope.
There is so much dark.

Having It All

Already you have half disappeared,
your limbs as thin as broom handles.

You sent me off to Tuscany
so you could shrink in silence
wanting me to live the life
you dreamt other people had,

but still I am the daughter of your austerity
caught in your habits of the Blitz
long after any real war was done.

I never saw you crease in laughter,
enjoy a ribald joke,
tuck into fattening food,
drink more than a bird's sip
of sherry.

And now you are propped
on your hospital bed
listening with deaf ears
to your favourite myth,
that the meek will inherit the earth.

How I want for you a different ending –

to see you rise like yeast
in the bread you used to knead,
full of zest, sap, juice, joy, certainty;
to have you shake your shoulders free,
stand tall and, with no apology,
looking neither back nor down,

jump with both feet
and claim it all:

the radiance,
the stars,
the full-fat light.

On Days Like This I Reach for Small Things

(i)
half-open snowdrops
bow from the side of the glass
sunlight in angles

(ii)
they nod their triumph
first frail signs of light returned
such provocation

(iii)
I take up a pen
work in a tentative way
sketch the white nuns' caps

(iv)
on their thin green stems
such quiet tenacity
the hours eternal

This Big Fat Moment
for Sophie Sabbage

I used to think time would get thin as it started
to run out, like a marathon runner gasping
for breath. But no, it grows fatter and fatter,
plumped up with the eternity to which it's heading.
Some days it's delicious as a doughnut,
and I lick sugar off the not-to-be-repeated morning,
the sky pink as papaya, nothing so sweet
as my young daughter's mouth
when she asks her innocent questions.
No more racing now towards an impossible future,
but each date gold-starred on the calendar
as if the sun had summoned it from darkness
just for us, the hours ripened into fat grapes,
days and nights Rubenesque with unexpected pleasure.
Moments stretch in the doorways of sleep,
seep into cracks between floorboards,
rise into the never-hurried mist of dawn.
Memories, past and imagined, cradle us
with their long arms, birthdays squat like candles
the wind cannot blow out. One second suddenly
swells with rapture, a brief sense of what-we're-here-for
inflates into whole libraries of meaning.
And I want to step with my child into the slowest,
slenderest hourglass, to make moments
that are too full to pass, our perfect now
become a house, a home she'll remember forever
as we face my disappearing –
this year, next year, sometime.

My Mother's Engagement Ring

Handed to me in a plastic bag
along with cash and wedding ring
this solitaire diamond

the tiny holes around the mount
which hold the diamond proud
clogged now with sediment.

For hours I scrub
with my inter-dental brush
prodding out the years

of standing at the sink,
the silt of soil, of soap,
of thread, of pastry dough,

tissues, hand-cream, widowhood,
thinking of all the things she touched
those last forty years

and all the things –
a man, a child, a glass of wine –
she didn't.

Persephone Blames the Dress

Everyone forgets the dress my mother made –
raw silk, its red the ember of dying skies.

Even as she stitched, fold after fold fell to the floor
like water seeking some underground pool.

She hung it on branches of sycamore
weighted the hems with poppy seeds.

As soon as I put it on, the earth quaked.
I slid my arms into cold mountain caves,

started at the flurry of bats, slipped on scree
disappearing between toppled birches.

The silk snagged as I pulled the neck down,
the whole thing too tight over my eyes

till I was falling, the whole world in darkness.
And the sound of something tearing.

Demeter Takes Up Embroidery

I spend my days sewing: fine golden stitches that shine in the darkness. I make pictures of plants she might have forgotten – thistles, acanthus, sea holly – to be ready for her when she returns. Note: I have erased the word *if* from my vocabulary.

Do not be taken in by this slenderness of thread. It holds as strong as spiders' silk, able to haul the dead from their graves. And as I work, I plan the adjustments I will make to my body.

Tiny running stitches to hold open the lids of my eyes, lest I miss the slightest glimpse of her in the distance. Larger stitches, herringbone, to close the passageway through which she entered the world.

I am done with all those seeds which breed loss.

5. A Room At Nightfall

Hilda, Unity and Dolls

following her divorce from Stanley Spencer, in 1942 Hilda
suffered a breakdown and spent time at Banstead Mental
Hospital, Surrey. 'Hilda Unity and Dolls' had been painted
by Spencer in 1937

Throw me at the wall.
I am carmine, carnelian,
cobalt, ultramarine.
I am soot, opaque pieces
of pigment trying to float their way
into his fat figures
of Christ
of Judas
to step back into that portrait
he did of the three of us –
me in grim-looking spectacles,
Unity and one of her dolls.
Unity.
The name didn't work.
We still split up.
I split up.

Think of me when you see him
pushing that black pram
round the streets of Cookham
laden with easels, canvas, oil.
That was my girls' pram.
It was their moat.
It was where they were rocked to sleep.

I could climb into it, my bones crushed
into paint, sepia coloured ash.
He could transform me
into one of his moon-faced saints.

Belonging to No One

It's the moving away from that moment
she remembers, more than the getting there.
Welsh mountains appearing in the train window,
white fields belonging to no one. Trying too hard
to please people from then on, as if she has a duty
to pour love in all the wrong places; drawn to others
who are inside out, showing their seams.
Not knowing if the father's single tear
was the sting of cold, or grief. Not knowing
if the child understood anything.

The kind of separation that makes it
impossible to stick maps together again;
the world, for all three of them now,
unhomely, incomplete.

Always that one day on a station platform,
the no man's land between Christmas and New Year,
when time departs down one track and she down another,
looking in railway carriages for suitcases, lost children,
that knitted bobble cap with its festive stripes,
his then smile.

The Girl Who Fell to Earth
on 8 May 1885, Sarah Ann Henley leapt from Clifton
Suspension Bridge in Bristol, but her crinoline skirts
carried her onto the banks

Every May, the rampant blossom taunts me.
Reminds me of that morning
when I floated high as a ship's mast
beneath Brunel's towers, my angry despair
somersaulting as public spectacle.

If I'd been a man, death's open arms
would have welcomed me,
but those silly petticoats
kept me alive – a cartoon angel
drifting from the skies.

The only others to survive this fall
were children: two girls whose soft bodies
impacted the mud and stayed intact,
their father – who'd lobbed them over –
outwitted as he looked down from the bridge.

I often dream I take them by the hand,
Ruby and Elsie, as if we've all three just landed
once more, and are drifting calmly downstream,
walking on water all the way to the Bristol Channel,
then out across a sea of fallen light.

Let There be Light

May the monsters never come.
May the street lamps be always on.
May there be a network of neon 24/7.
May we be visible from the space station.
May the brain stay alert, the red eye open.
May light, forever light, spread its pollution.
May we slow the leaving of the moon.
May we seize the blaze of the sun.
May we have no shadows, none
of the sable night that once was known
to bed our ancestors, to make the dawn
a miracle of things extinguished, new-born.

Visiting the Underworld, 1964

Rattling down in the cage
with my Dad
to those tunnels of hot darkness

where boys stripped to the waist
are casual smudges of charcoal
on half-lit walls

where tiny passageways
are lungs coated with soot
and the black roof rains phlegm

where we kneel on all fours
feeling our way
getting a taste of what real men do

while spirits of pit ponies
gallop towards fields
of couch grass vetch barley

and above our heads somewhere
Mum cooks Sunday roast
chops mint

says grace before dinner.

Like Orpheus

I came to you in the red dress you loved,
my skin oiled with summer, perfumed with jasmine.
I bribed the guards with snowflakes,
slipped easily through those seedy chinks
that lead downwards. And came ever deeper
till I reached your vanishing point.
Where you stood, still shocked,
disbelieving, as I threaded my warm hand
through your white arm and led you back upwards
towards those places still incandescent
with your light. I walked ahead, you followed,
a shadow in that land of shadows,
rising till the darkness grew less
as if bleach had been spilt into the ground
and black gave way to memories of blue.
That was when you noticed edges again –
one-way arrows pointing downwards –
and you remembered where you were
and stopped. I tried to urge you on with kisses,
promises of our usual pleasure,
explained how, with strong enough belief,
the doors between the worlds can open both ways.
I sang your favourite arias – Verdi, Monteverdi –
told you the old stories of how you can become more
as you become less. But already you were lost,
turned away from all I was trying to say,
locked back in certainties that kept your jaw stubborn,
your mind clinging to what it thought it knew.
And I knew then you were like Orpheus –
forever set on losing everything.

Song of Eurydice

If he could remember how I walked into a room
at nightfall, left off the lights so I could take him
in the dark, the darkness that opened us,
split us like a seam of coal.

If he could know how I hated neon,
that fluorescent weekend in Times Square,
how I might ride for hours on the Metro,
wanting a place where it's impossible to fall further.

If he could understand why I spurned theories
of relativity, didn't plan for the future,
wore little black dresses, dark glasses, had no mortgage,
felt most at home in crypt or cellar.

If he could stop exalting life over death,
the sleep of reason above earth's nascent dreams,
could let himself really taste the underworld
with its sap, heat, origins, extremes,

then he too might learn the necessity of descent,
step down into this country where love
makes of the darkness a dazzling thing –
not black space at all, but light that's full, blinding.

And so he need not lament his loss,
but tune his heartstrings to something
other than grieving, turn back to where
I stand in these shadows, hear my bones sing.

What the Ground Holds
i.m. Lucy Tisserand Rouse, 1976–2012

In the time it takes me to type her poem
she is gone, the room cleared
like one of Prospero's tricks.

I follow her to the high meadow
where birds fly up from startled grass
and saplings bow in the rain.

Her babies are here, their futures
changed forever by what this day holds,
what the ground opens to hold:

a willow casket drowned in petals
and this far too heavy earth
waiting to be shovelled back.

Beneath us, Somerset and Dorset
turn over their pages in the wind,
flimsy green maps, their contours shifting.

Lazarus

Fever was better than this,
a desert fever holding him high above the world
on burning coals.

Now he's cold, and though he juts his jaw
from side to side,
the darkness doesn't move.

He smells meat, rawness:
the underworld then, is that where he is, parcelled for death?
This pillow the pelvis of a stranger?

How he longs for light, just a slither
from the far side of that impossible stone;
craves it till he imagines fireflies,

then wedges of light so thick
they explode in a crash of yellow
breaking over his head.

Lazarus! As though from a lover, the word
strokes his skin, nudges him to clumsy feet.
Lazarus!

And he stumbles past the boulder
to a whole planet of light, yet not
the world he'd prayed for, after all,

for the fingers touching him are mere moth wings,
and there are no edges to things,
only eyes as fierce as suns staring into his,

luminous circles of flame,
his sisters lost in the radiance
and angels straddling the olive trees.

Garden of Olives
after Gauguin's 'Christ in the Garden of Olives', 1889

Not wanting that smell of rain on the horizon,
the too much light on his skin;

walking away from that tremor in the ground
where the remorseful dead inch towards him;

turning his back on the close ones
whose loyalty carries the sky for him;

yet unable to stop holding this world
as if he were cradling a bird in his arms,

the woman he has loved so much,
her knees on his chest, neck against his,

mouth by his ear, receiving everything
from her crouched beauty, whisper and kiss,

knowing he would rather break
than let her fall – choosing this.

Leonard Woolf at his Desk, 1940

My edges fit: there is no overlap.
I belong inside the tailored suit of myself.
She finds it more difficult to be contained,
to navigate the in and out of consciousness.

Each morning she has to work hard
to re-inhabit herself, pulls on layers of clothes
that are too cumbersome. At night
rehearses for the time she will disrobe herself entirely.

Most days, for all its size, the house is too small.
She paces the wooden floors like Alice,
longs to stick her arm up the chimney breast,
her elegant swan neck out of the window.

Always she out-writes me, leaves me sitting at my desk
when she's long finished her quota of words and slipped
outside, taken her body for a walk to the woods,
the river banks, as if it were a spaniel that needed exercise.

She watches herself, she tells me, as from high above the
    earth,
looking down on the unlikely blue and green of a strange
    planet.
Trapped in her tepid yet over-hot room, she arrives at a
    fullstop.
Steps outside again for a cool breath of air, another view
    of water.

This Dialogue Between the Dead and Living

I don't know how any of it works,
but this is how your passing comes to me.

Behold, you spend the night with me again,
pressing close, the whole house
filled with you.

You swim back the years, land us
in our unclouded time –
smiles for the camera,
hands clapping as you kiss me –
your tie the colour of my silk suit,
matching rings proof
of our diving to the depths,
finding the same treasure.

Once more you fasten flowers on the gate,
reach round my waist,
weigh in with promises –
the man you were –

and I can taste
the lost translucencies of things,
mistletoe strewn like pearls
amongst the apples.

But when I wake you're newly gone –
not, this time, to the woman you left me for –
but to a sea of glass and fire, the radiance
you're learning how to tread.

And I'm bereft a second time,
longing only to be there with you –
holding you, holding you,
both of us blinded
by the unaccustomed light.

6. Angels Of Rain And Light

Candle and Snow

after a 1957 letter by Stanley Spencer to his ex-wife, Hilda,
who had died in 1950

To say what is under a good layer of snow is difficult
the accident of my being here
you being there
snow falling with no regard for logic
falling over what went before

over all I meant to say
all that is difficult
its whiteness a trick
a new resting place
the shape on which softness will harden
the next layer to be walked upon

which is to say that love is difficult
the bridge between me here and you there
a new kind of courtship
a new *us*
with no regard for logic

the freshly falling
and the fallen on
a kind of snow.

Love Letters

Sometimes I dream my ex-husband writes to me
like Stanley Spencer wrote to Hilda, barely needing a reply
before his pen was off again, sending them both
to heaven, with St Peter on the Finchley Road lending his keys.

Our bedroom windows too are filled with birds and angels,
our morning cups of tea an early communion.
He writes me page after page, I am his woman in the moon,
his lost half of himself, his partner in an epic by Milton,

walking the pavement backwards to our earthly Paradise.
See how the fig leaves disappear, the awkwardness lost,
the kisses honey-filled once more, the me-you and you-me
translated back into a love before sorrow or war.

He will go on writing after my death, so obsessed with
who he finds himself to be in me, he barely notices
my body has disappeared, my coffin has no letter box.
And so he does not grieve at losing me,

but invites me to one of our long walks across the moor,
describes the May blossom, sketches it for a painting,
the profligate beauty ripe, improbable,
too rich for this world, too solid for the next.

My Own Heart Let Me Have More Pity On
after Gerard Manley Hopkins

You remember those nights when the roof of your house
didn't fit no matter where you lived, when you drove
out to the coast to contemplate darkness, the wind
on the cliff tops suitably bitter, the baggage
you carried dangerous and heavy. Dawn brought no
comfort, climbing down to houses where families
knew their rituals by heart, where the young faces
rushing out of doors were wet from showers of love.

Don't go back there now. Solace won't take root
with too much wandering. And though joy can't be forced,
you can trust it to arrive in its own unforeseen way,
like that sudden flight of swifts dipping and diving
round the eaves of your home, drawn to something they
     sense
there, some beauty, that you have yet to discover.

Margery Kempe and the Angel

When she prayed for Bliss
she didn't know
it would be this
bruising
didn't know   she'd be unable
to go back
to a horizontal kind of love
tender   fulfilled
her limbs as limp
and hands as loose
as fish   sleeping.

This is the vertical kind
doesn't let her rest
and   she needs to be held
needs the angel
who struck   to take her
under the armpits
grab her shoulders
stop her
collapsing
to the ground
weeping.

How could she have known
how rough Love is
how lonely
stretching
every sinew   every nerve
how strained   she would feel
by its attention
stained   by its beauty

longing   to rub out
          those dark shadows
     under her eyes?

How could she have known
               those wings
          would carry her
                    so far
     to where things
                    tear
     where   real light
          starts
               and blindness
     and seeing

                    are the same?

Living Into the Answers
i.m. Mirek Popowicz, 1952–2011

Needing to ask you the big questions.

Is silence there better than language here?
Do shadows really disappear?

Did Fiona meet you at the turnstile,
or did you have to enter the stadium of bones

to find her? Has she been given back her beauty?
Have you told her how you hung her wedding dress

on the back of the kitchen door,
so when you made soup you could talk to her?

Do you still write poems? In Polish or in English?
Why did you always use a fountain pen?

Are those camps of your childhood still with you?
The stroke that felled you? Do you miss your body

now it's stopped giving you pain?
Are you in bliss? What does suffering mean?

Do you remember chipmunks and cicadas?
What shall we do with the tiger skin?

Does Fiona remember the cancer that ate her?
Does she miss her face? Is there some secret to surrender?

Do you ever say *It was unfair?*

Mrs Thatcher Leaves Her Body and Meets
St Francis

Already the island is little more
than a shimmer of turquoise
beneath her

and though she has grown used to uncertainty
since her mind uncoupled itself,
still this rising unsettles her,

names slipping away further
till the light feels more like darkness,
coal dust, prayer turned upside down

and what is left travels to the place
where the soul sees what the mirror missed
and she calls out for the privilege

of picking up the crumbs under the table,
yearns to know what abasement is,
what love, what *caritas* –

asks to learn the life of birds.

The Three Finest Things God Ever Made According to Flaubert

1. Don Giovanni

Sitting in the old *teatro* in Cortona
watching all the bastards I have ever loved
get their comeuppance.
The charm of the man: his broad shoulders,
bass voice, commanding way he turns a woman's head,
that promise of deep pleasure in the eyes.
And the girl who is, of course, completely blameless,
relishing the flames of hell that lick across the stage
knowing the whole universe is on her side –
death invented for her innocence.

2. Hamlet

This, though, is what really happens
when vengeance gets the better of you:
more than one country counting the body bags,
corpses piling up.
Feigned madness skids too easily into the real thing –
a strait-jacket darkness –
Ophelia's herb-decked beauty drowned
while Rosencrantz and Guildenstern drift off-stage
with island mists closing in, gulls calling.

3. The Sea

At last, something beyond human contrivance –
the ocean – unbourgeois and unstoppable.
Element that escapes the hand,
that runs from thimbles, buckets, bodies, pipes,

ebbs in one flow from patterned surf
to depth, to dissolution and return.
See how it seams together earth and sky
with its blue vanishing point,
weaves its effortless way through us,
through stone.

Of Angels and Gender

You'd think I'd have learned their sex by now,
the way they squat in my house – painted, carved,
holding up the beams.

Yet when I put Masaccio's red-clothed angel
into a poem, and use the masculine pronoun,
my friend points out the angel's breasts,

the face of a long-haired Tuscan beauty. *Maybe*,
he says, *women think of them as men, and men
as women. Maybe they're the perfect love*

we dream of meeting. In Scripture, they're all male
– Gabriel, Michael, Lucifer – from seraphim
to outcast – *malak* – not a woman amongst them:

sandalled messengers of gods, who sit on clouds
of answers, too ready with dust and lilies
in their palms, handing out annunciations

with no sense of the morning sickness they lead to.
Not that I'm after an angel knitting her Bible
under an apple tree – one who casts off watery miracles,

unaware there can be too much light.
But give me a huge hermaphrodite – clothed in the sun,
with a skirt of thick gold, eyes that never close,

wings beating with the force of a hurricane,
their span enough to carry children out of sewers,
strong hands to hold us through our necessary fire.

Or then again, some eunuch who knows all about
missing buses, make-do love; knows that at least
three genders live under the surface of everything.

Not Falling

Not falling, but rising in love,
flying to where there's a view
and small miracles happen,
even lamp-posts burst into blossom.

The sky full of swallows, red kites, jays,
their feathers drifting blue and scarlet
into our picnic laps,
our tongues inventing new soubriquets.

All those days of well-rehearsed solitude
squandered by this unlooked-for visitation,
this new tenderness in the air,
not one drop of champagne wasted.

After the Door Has Opened

*the shrine of Hazrat Babajan, a Muslim 'Perfect Master', is
in the Char Bawdi district of Pune, India. Until her death
in 1931, Babajan spent her last 24 years living here under a
neem tree and, in 1913, revealed to Meher Baba his spiritual
identity*

Here, in San Jan Mohammad Street,
dwells she who is no longer she,
whose desire is gone, who waits
for what is already done.

She is *Hafizah* –
one who has learned the Koran by heart.
She has visited the black box at Mecca,
kissed the stone of the Kaaba,
but she chooses the holy slums of Pune,
where hunger shrivels in unshaded heat.

Women break at her feet their coconuts of prayer,
make their supplications for babies.
But she knows the gift of sorrow –
how we may learn to squeeze sugar
out of grief.

She knows walking is always backwards,
the best living a kind of erasure –
each day rubbing out the folly of what went before;
how the greatest millstone of pain
cannot grind the grain of you small enough,
the finest sieve will not make you pure.

Her hair is the white of egrets.
Her face *Gulrukh* – like a rose.
And since the time her life opened
onto the fire that gives God his heat,
she knows the deceit of daylight.

So what if she was Rabia of Basra,
who wrote pleasure in the sand?
She would rather be despised as the thief
who climbed in to steal her final blanket.
Even the best poems should not be worshipped,
but hung out like rags. Words must buckle
at the knees.

Yes, here, in San Jan Mohammad Street,
trades a stallkeeper from whom few want to buy.
Her age – a hundred or more –
small matter as she sits
under the angel of the neem tree
seven centuries between each feather.

John Donne Arriving in Heaven

He knew it would be a melting, looking back
at the world as a place of icicles and clouds,
lilies of passion unmooring their tangled roots.

Knew that with the rungs of prayer and reason
knocked away, the subtle knot undone,
he would step into this delicate permanence,

the light cleansing, as protracted evening sun
perfects a field of harvest corn.
Expected such radiance that finds no flaws

in all that's happened, no severity,
only the mercy of a paradise always autumn,
its joy possessed, ripe, perfect, complete.

But this is less the arrival he foresaw
than an undoing of distances, a shedding
of himself to become who he already was,

not gaining union but losing the illusion
he was separate, was ever other than this one:
the hand that set all things in motion,

spread this equal light, made on a whim
the stars, the schoolboys, the unruly sun.
All love a dream of this. And now, as he takes on

the bliss, the infinite bliss his little deaths
on earth struggled to reach, he finds his words
at last translated to their proper tongue.

Later

we remembered
what we had put away
and thought we had lost

the small blessings
the gratitude
too easy to forgo

and as we unpacked them
that afternoon
shaking out creases

removing moth balls
we marvelled at the simplicity
the way everything felt

it was happening
for the first time
which of course

after the carelessness
between us
it was

Resurrection
after Stanley Spencer, 'The Resurrection: Reunion', 1945

And suddenly they are streaming back from the dead,
unburying themselves,
their tombstones mere props for gossip
now the final day has come.

Only this is not the last day,
but the first of an eternal summer
where loss turns back into desire,
for what can match the pleasure of a kiss
on the tongue of those grown accustomed to tasting nothing?

Nothing more glorious for those whose senses were lost
than these arms around the loved one's shoulder,
the conjugal embrace, the breasts
that never bruise with too much touching,
the heavy angels spilling out of windows and doors
to welcome them home.

This is what they dreamt of ascending to –
gardens, allotments, lamps pooling light over dinner.
This what they longed to recapture –
reaching round a chest that rises and falls,
the rapture of breath that doesn't stop.

Flesh ripe with joy now they are touching again –
lovers, mothers, children, fathers, plumped-up wives –
in this light that is never switched off,
these bodies that cannot have enough of each other,
this love that is always being made.

Acknowledgements

You can hear me reading many of the poems from *The Light Box* online at www.soundcloud.com and www.macguffin.io.

Some of these poems first appeared in: *Acumen, Domestic Cherry, The Frogmore Papers, Poetry Salzburg Review, Scintilla, Tears in the Fence, The Interpreter's House,* online in *The Fat Damsel;* Templar's *Peloton* Anthology (2013); *The Listening Walk* (2013); *Ghost Notes* (2015); *Salt on the Wind,* an anthology of poems in tribute to Ruth Stone (2015); and my pamphlet *What The Ground Holds* (Poetry Salzburg, 2014). 'The Desire to be Porcelain' was written for an anthology of poetry and art edited by Frances-Anne King, for Holburne Museum, Bath as part of their centenary celebrations, 2016.

Thank you to Coleman Barks for generous permission to use his translation of one of Lalla's poems for the epigraph, taken from *Naked Song* (Maypop Books, 1992).

'John Donne Arriving in Heaven' won Joint First Prize in the Bath Poetry Café competition 2015, judged by Rachel Boast; 'Spoons' was given the Hilly Cansdale award by Peter Oswald in the Wells Poetry Competition 2015; 'The Light Box' won Second Prize in the Battered Moons Poetry Competition 2015, judged by Pascale Petit; 'Mary Shelley, Hyde Park, 1850', was Highly Commended at Torbay in 2015; 'First Breakfast' was shortlisted in the Bridport Poetry Competition 2015; 'Night Sky' was shortlisted by Martin Malone for the Bradford on Avon Festival Poetry competition 2014; 'The Lovers' Exchange' won Second Prize in the Havant Festival Poetry Competition 2013, judged by Wendy Klein; 'Resurrection' won Second Prize in the Acumen and Bath Poetry Café competition 2102, judged by Patricia Oxley.

An earlier version of 'On Days Like This' was made into a copper sculpture by Andrew Whittle for the grounds of Glendinning Health Unit on Maiden Castle Road, Dorchester, in 2011.

I am deeply grateful to Claire Dyer for her supportive mentoring and editing; to Dawn Gorman and Claire Crowther for excellent critiques; to the Frome Poetry Society Stanza Group; the Knucklebones and Subversifs poetry groups in Bath; and to Rosie Bailey, William Bedford, Jo Bell, Stephen Boyce, Lindsay Clarke, Rachael Clyne, David Davies, Lyn Davies, Rose Flint, Robert Lee, Gordon McKerrow, Crysse Morrison, Jay Ramsay, Lesley Saunders, Francis Spencer and many others who are part of the wonderfully vibrant network of poets in the South West.

Several of these poems began in workshops led by Roselle Angwin, Sue Boyle, Carrie Etter, Philip Gross, Jenny Lewis, Tim Liardet, Pascale

Petit, Hilda Sheehan. Thank you to them all. Also to Saber Khan at Toppings Bookshop, Bath and to Maria C. McCarthy and Bob Carling at Cultured Llama.

Praise for *What The Ground Holds*, by Rosie Jackson

These are fluid, eloquent poems, and Rosie Jackson has an emotional range which encompasses tragedy as well as curiosity and delight.

Helen Dunmore

Like the image of Virginia Woolf watching her life 'as from high above the earth,/looking down on the unlikely green and blue of a strange planet', these poems hang in a delicate balance between felt immediacy and a wider perspective sharply aware of time and passing ... even when that transience is made permanent by myth or art. Far from distancing them, this perspective lights the scenes with a tender intensity.

Philip Gross

These poems are exquisite, delicate strength created through precise wording and profound feeling. Classic myths glimmer through contemporary experiences, and the ordinary becomes unfamiliar and scarred with legend.

Crysse Morrison

There is a restrained anguish throughout *What the Ground Holds* ... A marvellous collection.

William Bedford, *Ink, Sweat and Tears*

Everywhere this poet bridges the gap between the ancient and the modern; between the real and the imagined. Although many of these poems are saturated with death and loss, they are assembled with utter beauty, both original and controlled – a truly remarkable feat.

Wendy Klein, *London Grip*

Poems as delicate and strong as spiders' silk.

Alison Brackenbury

Cultured Llama Publishing
Poems | Stories | Curious Things

Cultured Llama was born in a converted stable. This creature of humble birth drank greedily from the creative source of the poets, writers, artists and musicians that visited, and soon the llama fulfilled the destiny of its given name.

Cultured Llama aspires to quality from the first creative thought through to the finished product.

www.culturedllama.co.uk

Also published by Cultured Llama

Poetry

strange fruits by Maria C. McCarthy
Paperback; 72pp; 203×127mm; 978-0-9568921-0-2; July 2011

A Radiance by Bethany W. Pope
Paperback; 70pp; 203×127mm; 978-0-9568921-3-3; June 2012

The Strangest Thankyou by Richard Thomas
Paperback; 98pp; 203×127mm; 978-0-9568921-5-7; November 2012

The Night My Sister Went to Hollywood by Hilda Sheehan
Paperback; 82pp; 203×127mm; 978-0-9568921-8-8; March 2013

Notes from a Bright Field by Rose Cook
Paperback; 104pp; 203×127mm; 978-0-9568921-9-5; July 2013

Sounds of the Real World by Gordon Meade
Paperback; 104pp; 203×127mm; 978-0-9926485-0-3; August 2013

The Fire in Me Now by Michael Curtis
Paperback; 90pp; 203×127mm; 978-0-9926485-4-1; August 2014

Short of Breath by Vivien Jones
Paperback; 102pp; 203×127mm; 978-0-9926485-5-8; October 2014

Cold Light of Morning by Julian Colton
Paperback; 90pp; 203×127mm; 978-0-9926485-7-2; March 2015

Automatic Writing by John Brewster
Paperback; 96pp; 203×127mm; 978-0-9926485-8-9; July 2015

Zygote Poems by Richard Thomas
Paperback; 66pp; 178×127mm; 978-0-9932119-5-9; July 2015

Les Animots: A Human Bestiary by Gordon Meade, images by Douglas Robertson
Hardback; 166pp; 203×127mm; 978-0-9926485-9-6; December 2015

Memorandum: Poems for the Fallen by Vanessa Gebbie
Paperback; 90pp; 203×127mm; 978-0-9932119-4-2; February 2016

Short stories

Canterbury Tales on a Cockcrow Morning by Maggie Harris
Paperback; 138pp; 203×127mm; 978-0-9568921-6-4; September 2012

As Long as it Takes by Maria C. McCarthy
Paperback; 168pp; 203×127mm; 978-0-9926485-1-0; February 2014

In Margate by Lunchtime by Maggie Harris
Paperback; 204pp; 203×127mm; 978-0-9926485-3-4; February 2015

The Lost of Syros by Emma Timpany
Paperback; 128pp; 203×127mm; 978-0-9932119-2-8; July 2015

Curious things

Digging Up Paradise: Potatoes, People and Poetry in the Garden of England by Sarah Salway
Paperback; 164pp; 203×203mm; 978-0-9926485-6-5; June 2014

Punk Rock People Management: A No-Nonsense Guide to Hiring, Inspiring and Firing Staff by Peter Cook
Paperback; 40pp; 210×148mm; 978-0-9932119-0-4; February 2015

Do it Yourself: A History of Music in Medway by Stephen H. Morris
Paperback; 504pp; 229×152mm; 978-0-9926485-2-7; April 2015

The Music of Business: Business Excellence Fused with Music by Peter Cook – NEW EDITION
Paperback; 318pp; 210×148mm; 978-0-9932119-1-1; May 2015

The Hungry Writer by Lynne Rees
Paperback; 246pp; 244×170mm; 978-0-9932119-3-5; September 2015

The Ecology of Everyday Things by Mark Everard
Hardback; 126pp; 216×140mm; 978-0-9932119-6-6; November 2015

Printed in April 2021
by Rotomail Italia S.p.A., Vignate (MI) - Italy